HOW TO BE AN EXPERT WITNESS

ABOUT THE AUTHORS

Dennis Merenbach is admitted to practice law in all courts in California, the United States Supreme Court, and many courts of the Federal Circuit. He is a member of Public Investor's Arbitration Bar Association. He received his bachelor's degree from the University of Southern California, and his Juris Doctor from Loyola Law School at Los Angeles. He completed the National College of Advocacy at Harvard Law School. He attended St. James College in Oxford, England. Mr. Merenbach started practicing law in 1966. His office is currently in Santa Barbara, California. He has been a consultant on all matters of trial for the television soap operas "Santa Barbara" and "The Guiding Light." His litigation experience includes cases in Business Law, Securities Arbitration, Personal Injury, Contracts, and Criminal in both state and federal courts. He is also the host of the weekly radio program, "You and the Law" on KTMS-AM in Santa Barbara.

Anthony Stephen has degrees in political science and law. While in law school, Mr. Stephen was awarded the American Jurisprudence Prize for excellence in both the *Law of Evidence and Criminal Law* by Bancroft-Whitney Co. and The Lawyers Co-Operative Publishing Co., joint publishers of the Annotated Reports System. He has worked in the construction project and contract management fields both domestically and abroad the past thirty-five years. His career includes dealing with people from all walks of life in many unique situations. Additionally, he has written and edited many manuals and several books.

How To Be An Expert Witness

Credibility in Oral Testimony

By

DENNIS G. MERENBACH,
ATTORNEY AT LAW,

AND

ANTHONY STEPHEN,
B.S., LL.B.

FITHIAN PRESS
SANTA BARBARA
1993

Design and typography by Jim Cook

Published by Fithian Press
a division of Daniel & Daniel, Publishers, Inc.
Post Office Box 1525
Santa Barbara, California 93102

LIBRARY OF CONGRESS CATALOGING-IN-PUBLICATION DATA
Merenbach, Dennis G., 1934–
How to be an expert witness: credibility in oral testimony
Dennis G. Merenbach & Anthony Stephen.
p. cm.
ISBN 1-56474-048-X
1. Witnesses—United States.
I. Stephen, Anthony. II. Title.
KF8950.M47 1993
347.73'67—dc20
[347.30767] 92-35863
CIP

To my parents,
Walter and Eula Merenbach

To my sons,
Anthony and Timothy Stephen

❦

Special thanks to Dr. Craig R. Smith for his valuable
comments and editorial review of the manuscript.
Dr. Smith is Professor and Chairman of the
Department of Communications,
California State University, Long Beach

Contents

Preface

This book is *not* a primer on the law of evidence. The information contained herein serves as a set of reminders to persons who may be called upon to function as expert witnesses in a courtroom, arbitration, or some type of administrative hearing. It is also intended to be a practical guideline for laymen as well as a refresher for the professional.

Important reminders are highlighted in **bold type.** The reminders are accompanied by simple cartoons and descriptive captions. We may have accidentally omitted some important reminders; however, we think that if the reader digests most of the material in this book, he or she will be a competent expert witness. The terms "he" and "she" are used generically throughout the book and we hope this use will not offend the reader.

This book is small enough to be carried in a pocket, purse, or handbag. Note that the reminders are also printed at the back of the book under the heading POINTS TO REMEMBER.

This book is divided into two parts. The first part describes what an expert witness is and many of the common experiences the witness may have. It was considered necessary to acquaint the layman with an idea of this segment of the law of evidence. That is, a person (under oath) sitting in front of an audience and trying to tell the truth as he or she perceives it. The second part describes the important points to remember.

References to the first person in the body of this book include some personal experiences of Mr. Merenbach during his practice of law. Anecdotes by Mr. Merenbach are sprinkled throughout the text to more fully illustrate important points.

Part I
Defining an Expert Witness

What is an Expert Witness?

*I never could tell a lie that anybody would doubt,
nor a truth that anybody would believe.*

—MARK TWAIN

Every person is an expert witness: people from every stratum of life, every occupation, job, or hobby on any subject matter qualify as experts. The busboy is an expert witness on how to handle his job. His observations on what he can see in a restaurant *or* kitchen is from a different perspective than that of a customer, a waiter, a chef, a cashier, the maître de, or the owner of the establishment.

The expert witness cuts across every segment and fragment of our society, because with each person comes the unique ability to see life from his or her own unique position. In short, all people are experts about themselves and their jobs. The reason you are being called as an expert witness is because your testimony will honestly support the object of the attorney on your side of the case.

What is an expert witness? **An expert witness is one whose testimony, or whose observations, communicate special knowledge that the average person does not have.**

Expert witnesses can interpret certain acts or facts in a given field. To put it another way, an expert is a specialist. You can be a specialist on traffic flow in your neighborhood as well as a specialist in microbiology.

I remember when an over-the-road truck driver was on the witness stand. At first he testified as to weather conditions, the fact that the pavement was dry, and it was a four-lane road divided by a double yellow line. At that point, a number of questions were asked of the truck driver on the speed of the other vehicles. Objections were properly made. Unless he had specialized knowledge or experience, he couldn't testify as to speed. The truck driver immediately answered the question by saying, "Any man who is an over-the-road truck driver is an expert in estimating the speed of oncoming as well as outgoing vehicles."

Upon further inquiry, a determination was made that the truck driver had been driving for twenty-five years over the road. As part of his experience, he had had the opportunity to time different vehicles. He had been able to coordinate this timing with observation of vehicles moving from one point to another. He had done this in such a manner that he had gained the expertise to correlate a visual sense of speed with a clock. Thus, this truck driver qualified as an expert witness on the speed of vehicles involved in an accident.

This example leads to a second important point about being an expert witness. We must *prepare* any person who is going to relate to an incident, a factual situation, or his opinion. This preparation will have an impact upon those

[14]

who are to be persuaded; that is, who are to **believe** the witness. If it is a courtroom trial, or a peer group session, or a group of his peers on certifying him for some specialized function, the witness must be prepared so he is believable.

The witness is no more than an individual who relates facts that he observed, facts that he knows to be true because of his experience and education. He must relate these facts in a credible (believable) manner. *Credibility, according to Aristotle and several modern psychologists, is based on character, goodwill, expertise, spontaneity and congruence (consistency).*

This witness may come to the courtroom in fear that in some way or other there will be personal attacks on him, and an attempt to discredit him either personally or professionally, and with the fear that he will be exposed and ridiculed, and will face rejection because his testimony was not accepted. These fears can be alleviated by (1) **knowledge**, (2) **rehearsal**, and (3) **experience**. The above three points aid in preparing an expert witness.

The most experienced witnesses I've met are law enforcement officers, doctors, and appraisers. They routinely testify on a *weekly* basis. This routine testimony is needed for courtroom resolution of anything from a simple automobile stopped for speeding to the most serious and heinous crimes that were ever committed. So the police officer, after being on the job for two or three years, gains considerable experience in handling the most common questions asked of him. His memory is tested when he faces those who try to impeach his testimony and character. The experience of the law enforcement officer is seldom matched by any non-law enforcement person.

The **reminders** in this document are those usually practiced by most **law enforcement individuals, doctors, appraisers, engineers, scientists, and analysts when they are expert witnesses.**

If you are called upon to give testimony on your behalf, or on behalf of someone else, or on a technical subject, you must be prepared with the knowledge of an expert witness. The likelihood is that this will be the first time you have ever given such testimony. It is difficult to have developed any practice or experience before first taking the witness stand unless you are prepared by rehearsal.

As its basic goal, this book seeks to overcome that absolute, paralyzing fear that can occur in a person when he hears the words, "Jones, please take the witness stand."

There was one case where I could see fear in the eyes of the engineer. He was called by my opponent *without* preparation or rehearsal. His nervousness could be seen in the way he wrung his hands and constantly rubbed his nose. When asked a question he covered his lips with his finger. I learned he had written a report two years before but had not reviewed it. When my time came to examine him, I held the report in my hand so he could see it. I asked him questions as though I were reading from the pages of the report. He answered in the affirmative to all the questions. Each affirmative answer destroyed his testimony. **He couldn't know I was *not* asking questions based on the report; thus, his *credibility was destroyed.***

For some areas of endeavors, one must understand the definition of the word **"science."** A meaning of the word is a systematized knowledge derived from observation, study, and experimentation carried on by determining the nature or principles of what is being studied. Contrast the definition of science to that of art, which can be considered the disposition or modification of things by human skill, to answer the purpose intended, which generally involves creative work or its principles.

Art, as distinguished from science, leads one to a definition of craft, some special art, or some special skill.

Another way to distinguish between science and art is that science is objective and unbiased and conforms to reality. Art is based on generative (creative) principles that have exceptions. It is subjective and does not conform to reality, but seeks to idealize it. **A *scientist* like Carl Sagan can testify about the stars as an expert; Van Gogh, the *artist* who painted "Starry Night," could not.**

Medicine, for example, is best analyzed as an applied science in that it uses actual practice to work out practical problems. This illustration distinguishes applied science from pure abstract and theory. Opinion is a belief not based on absolute certainty or positive knowledge but on what is true, valid, or probable in one's mind, or what one thinks or what one judges. Aristotle refers to this as "true opinion" as opposed to "inartistic proof."

Why or how do experts appear to be so far apart on their opinions? Lawyers suspect, cast reasonable doubt, cross examine, probe, discredit, and search for the facts to which the law can be applied. They meet people who practice deception on a daily basis.

Lawyers are accustomed to the lying and unreliable lay witness who cannot give an accurate, believable (credible) report on facts he allegedly perceives. When it is desired that an expert give facts, these facts are an *opinion* of the witness.

General Considerations

Preparing the Witness for Examination

The lawyer should prepare each witness he intends to call to testify truthfully, accurately, and credibly. The testimony should be such that the trier of fact will listen, understand, remember, and believe it. Attorneys are constantly amazed by what a jury remembers during deliberation. A juror cannot remember what he can't hear. The following story illustrates this point.

My expert on handwriting analysis was on the stand. She testified as to her educational credentials and why she had been allowed to testify as an expert. I looked at the jury and noticed three jurors nodding off in the warm courtroom. *I dropped the book I was holding and everyone sat up and focused one hundred percent attention on the witness.*

Question: Is the handwriting the same?
Answer: Yes.

That was all I wanted the jurors to remember in the jury room. It took the jury only thirty-five minutes to bring in a verdict for my client.

This document will help you in your capacity as an expert witness. In these litigious days and times the scope of courtroom and administrative hearings is likely to increase rather than decrease.

Advice to the Expert Witness. In your capacity as an expert witness, *your function is to be honest and believable.* The law has placed a clear duty on the presiding officer and your lawyers to protect you from mistreatment.

The laws provide that it is the right of a witness to be protected from irrelevant, improper, or insulting questions, from harassment, and from harsh or insulting demeanor. The laws also provide for examination only on matters legal and pertinent to the issues. As much as possible, your lawyers will try to protect you in this area. However, it is difficult for your lawyer to protect you unless you discuss your fears with him beforehand. As a witness helping the trier of fact, you contribute to the maintenance and usefulness of one of the greatest institutions devised by civilization for the ascertainment of truth. **Your contribution to this process is worthy of your best efforts.**

The *attitude* you display to the court usually has an important effect on the credibility of your testimony. Experts who are highly trained in technical areas often have problems communicating with juries. **They (the experts) have an elevated professional pride and always give the impression that their time is extremely valuable.** They resent any challenge by a layman or a person who is not an expert. It is not unusual for them to display hostilities toward lawyers and all things legal. *When you testify, don't create this type of impression. It will negatively affect your credibility and ability to be persuasive with a trier of fact.*

You may or may not be sworn as a witness. If you have any religious or anti-religious scruples about "swearing," that is, a moral aversion toward taking an oath, make the fact known to your attorney.

If he does not so inform the presiding officer, you may personally state your position. The presiding official will then order the clerk to recite to you an affirmation under penalty of perjury which you will confirm by your answer "I do." It will not be necessary for you to inform the presiding official or your lawyer of the reason for your scruple, for example, that you are an atheist, a member of a certain religious sect, or of any other persuasion.

In most jurisdictions the oath is stated as "Do you swear or affirm to tell the truth"; this wording removes the problem of moral conscience.

Speak slowly, clearly, and distinctly—not with exaggerated force but sufficiently loud to be heard by the trier of fact. Speak with fluency and vocal variety; you must *sound* sincere. You do not have to speak for people beyond the barrier. You are not called as an adversary or an advocate but rather to carry on a *discussion*, albeit with a little more vocal power than you use in your living room or private office. The above rules of vocal delivery in a legal or quasi-legal environment can only be successfully achieved through constant practice — as noted with the testimony of professional witnesses discussed above.

Types of Questions

There are at least three types of questions an adverse attorney may ask a witness. One is a general type requiring a *narrative* answer. A second is a *leading* question suggesting to the witness the answer desired by the examiner. A third type is a *hypothetical* question reciting facts and other matter on which an expert witness is asked to base his opinion testimony.

Narrative Answers. A narrative answer is one in which you as a witness respond at length to a general question. This is in contrast to stating individual facts by reconstructing an event, or answering a series of specific questions. You are permitted to tell your story in your own words (do so with continuity), uninterrupted by the panel or opposing attorney.

If your testimony is favorable, and you can express yourself clearly and logically, little is gained by the examiner keeping a close question-answer rein on you. Specific questions can later be directed to you on any points you fail to mention or emphasize.

Narrative answers are not always advantageous. If you are nervous or your thoughts are not well organized, a narrative answer can be rambling and confusing. You might utter harmful testimony, use phraseology that conveys a wrong impression, or state inadmissible matter that causes interruption because of an objection or motion to strike. An effective way to provide a narrative answer is like telling a story. Start from the beginning and follow through in chronological order. *However, always keep in mind that you should recite only the relevant facts.*

Leading Questions. A leading question suggests to the witness the answer desired by the examiner. Sometimes, leading questions are intentionally asked to keep the flow of testimony smooth and interesting, and to help you keep your answers relevant, responsive, and complete. Leading questions are not allowed on direct examination. However, they are allowed on cross-examination. Therefore, during direct examination you cannot be asked:

Q. Were you standing on Main St. and 2nd at
   2 P.M. on July 20, 1985?

Instead, you will be asked:

Q. Where were you at 2 P.M. on July 20, 1985?

The leading question is permitted on cross-examination.

A question is not leading simply because it can be answered "yes" or "no." It is leading if it suggests that the answer is "yes" rather than "no," or vice versa. A leading question is not automatically converted into a non-leading form by such words as "State whether or not . . . , " "if any," or "if at all," although these words may save a few questions from objection.

Hypothetical Questions. Hypothetical questions recite facts and other matter on which an expert witness is asked to base his opinion testimony. The witness is asked to assume, for the purposes of his or her answer, that the matter recited in the question is true, whether or not the expert has any knowledge of that matter, even though the expert may believe it to be false. The matter on which the expert's opinion is based is thus "made known" during the hearing.

The use of hypothetical questions has been much criticized, but they have not been abolished and are still employed to elicit and test expert opinion testimony.

A fact recited in a hypothetical question may be disputed. The question is proper if there is some evidence to sustain the recited fact, if the fact is reasonably inferred from the evidence, or if it is within the possible or probable range of the evidence.

In formulating a hypothetical question, a person has considerable latitude to select the facts that support one's theory of the case and to omit the facts that favor one's opponent.

Hypothetical questions must contain facts already in evidence. For example, 30 feet of skid marks, glass on the street, and damage to the car—all of which evidence could help form an expert's opinion as to speed. The question would be as follows:

Assume these facts.

1. The white car left 30 feet of skid marks.
2. Glass was located at the end of the skid marks.
3. The front end damage to the white car was extensive.
Q. Having all these facts in mind, can you give an opinion as to the speed of the white car?

An objection to a hypothetical question should point out specific deficiencies and should be made in time to give the examiner an opportunity to correct the question.

Hypothetical questions are used to supply information to an expert witness lacking personal knowledge of an event, instrumentality, or person about whom the expert is to testify, and as a convenient means of summarizing and restating all matter that supports the opinion to be delivered by the witness. These types of questions are almost always used with every expert witness such as an accident reconstruction specialist, pathologist, arson investigator, auditor, analyst, or engineer.

The following dialogue shows some of the ways in which a hypothetical question could be used on direct examination:

> Q. Please answer your next questions on the basis of the following facts: (Recite all facts). Did you familiarize yourself with these facts and the information before coming here today?
>
> A. Yes, I did.
>
> Q. Based upon those facts, have you (concluded/ reached a judgment/formed an opinion/etc.) whether . . . ?
>
> A. I have.
>
> Q. Please state your conclusion.
>
> A. . . . .
>
> Q. What are the reasons for your conclusion?
>
> A. (You may give your analysis and synthesis of the information, and point out matters of particular significance.)

Note: An example of the above was provided in the white car damage case described earlier.

Hypothetical questions are used to gain favorable opinion testimony from an opposing examiner, and to gain an admission that his opinion would be different if the witness were to base it on different assumptions. These types of questions are also used to test the witness' accuracy, competency, or credibility.

In constructing a hypothetical question to ask an expert, the adverse examiner will draw from the evidence a set of facts that will urge a fair-minded expert to give an answer consistent with the adverse examiner's theory. The witness can be told to assume these facts by answering the question, even though the witness might believe them to be untrue and has already given a contrary opinion based on different matter. The adverse examiner will avoid using data that the trier of fact is unlikely to believe.

The best situation is often the one in which the expert continues to accept all the matter that the expert's original opinion was based on, but is also asked to consider new information supplied by the examiner. If the examiner can convince the court or the panel that the facts recited in the examiner's hypothetical question are more complete and accurate, the opinion given by the expert may prevail over a previous opinion.

Types of Witnesses

Lay Witnesses. A lay witness may testify to facts only, and generally is not permitted to give an opinion. An opinion is an inference from facts observed. **One of the fundamental rules of the law of evidence is that lay witnesses must testify as to facts only, leaving inferences or conclusions to the judge or jury.**

Expert Witnesses. A person who is an expert witness may express an opinion in his or her field of expertise. You are qualified to testify as an expert if you have special

knowledge, skill, experience, training, or education suffi-
cient to qualify you as an expert on the subject to which the
testimony relates. An expert witness may not express an
opinion outside his or her field of expertise.

You "testify as an expert" when you:

(1) testify in the form of an opinion on a subject that is
beyond common experience;

(2) state the reasons for your opinion and the data on
which it is based, which may include material not
personally known;

(3) testify about facts that laymen would be incapable
of perceiving, comprehending, or describing.

The reasons for eliciting a witness' special qualifications
are:

(1) to qualify you to testify as an expert;

(2) to show part of the material on which your opinion
testimony is based;

(3) to support your credibility; and

(4) to provide a factual basis for arguing the superiority
of your qualifications over those of opposing experts.

Holding a professional license or a college degree does not
necessarily qualify a witness as an expert, **nor does the
lack of a license, degree, or formal education automatically disqualify you from being an expert.**

**An example is the case of product liability where
glass was found in a bottle of wine. The witness called
to the stand to explain the bottling process was a fore-
man on the bottling line. He did not have a high school
education, but was knowledgeable in the entire technical method of operation.**

An expert witness can testify in the form of an opinion if

the opinion is related to a subject that is sufficiently beyond common experience that an expert's opinion would assist the trier of fact.

Your opinion testimony must be based upon a conclusion that you have reached. As an expert you can base your opinion, in part, on the opinions of other experts, but you cannot simply repeat another's opinion as your own on no other basis than reliance on the other person's judgment. Nor can the expert give an opinion that is nothing more than the consensus of a committee, group, or "experts in the field."

Expert opinion testimony is limited to subjects that are beyond the competence of persons of common experience, training, and education. A witness could be prevented from testifying in expert opinion form if the subject were one of such common knowledge that the conclusion could be reached by persons of ordinary education. As a practical matter, however, there are few topics in which some persons are not better educated and more experienced than others.

The opinion of a witness testifying as an expert must be based on matters of a type that reasonably may be relied upon. **"Matters"** include any conceivable basis for an opinion: e.g., facts, dates, the witness' knowledge and experience, and other intangibles. An expert can base an opinion on a matter made known to the witness at or before the hearing, as well as on matter perceived by or personally known to the expert.

For example, it is reasonable for a doctor to rely on a report given him by another doctor, but it is not reasonable for an accident investigator determining a point of impact to rely solely on the statements of bystanders. Both state-ments are hearsay—one is a proper basis for opinion testi-mony whereas the other is not.

Similarly, expert opinion testimony cannot be based on irrelevant or speculative matter, not because those matters are inadmissible, but because it is not reasonable for experts to rely on such matter.

A witness testifying in the form of an opinion may state the reasons for his/her opinion and the matter upon which it is based. There does not seem to be any practical distinc-tion between "reasons" and "matters." Taken together, they permit you to testify about the sources from which you de-rived the facts and information that influenced your conclu-sion, including the application of analysis, logic, and judg-ment to the facts and information under consideration.

Detailed testimony from an expert witness about the matter on which the expert's opinions are based, and the reasons for them, tends to support, explain, and give im-pact to the expert's testimony.

Part II
Important Reminders

General Conduct

REMINDER NO. 1. Dress in good taste, as you would dress to go to church, temple, or an important business function. Flamboyant or inappropriate attire detracts from the desired impression. Suit coats and ties are appropriate clothes for men. Conservative suits or dresses are appropriate clothes for women; excessive makeup or jewelry should be avoided. Modesty, neatness, and dignity should be displayed. Chewing gum or other edibles is an activity construed by many to connote disrespect, so it must be avoided.

Dress in good taste!

REMINDER NO. 2. Be thoroughly honest in your intent and speech; only for that purpose are you called as a witness. The most honest witness, however, can accidentally err through failure of memory or confusion. **If testimony includes a recital of numbers, be sure to doublecheck the arithmetic; have your charts proofread.** If you should come to realize that you did err in any testimony, admit and correct your error at your first opportunity. If this opportunity should not present itself in your examination, tell the presiding official that you want to change certain testimony. You may speak during a recess to your attorney; tell him of your mistake and he will see that it is corrected.

Make an effort to understand precisely the question put to you and answer only that particular question. Understand what lies behind the question. Answer it fully, but go no further.

Dodging or evading the question is negative. Arguing with the examiner must be avoided at all costs. If you don't understand the question, *courteously* ask the examiner if he or she would mind reframing the question.

Be thoroughly honest in your intent and speech.

You may be pressed to give a "yes" or "no" answer or an answer that, in your judgment, would convey a half truth or a wrong impression. You may feel that the answer, without some elaboration, would be unfair to yourself, or to another witness. The questioner is entitled to a yes-or-no answer; however, after you answer yes or no, state to the examiner or to the presiding officer that you wish to explain your answer or supplement it, or express your thought about the matter.

Remain calm if an attorney moves to strike out your remarks or gets excited about your speeches. If the presiding official wants to hear the whole truth, he will be fair and will make a proper ruling or suggestion. If he thinks you are "making speeches," being irrelevant, arguing, or doing anything else that is improper, he will admonish you. Never hesitate to say, "I'm sorry, Judge" (or "Mr. Chairman," or the appropriate title of the official) if you feel the statement is appropriate.

REMINDER No. 3. Resolve to be the master of the situation. Keep your emotions under firm control regardless of how tiresome, trivial, abusive, or unnecessary you may think the examination has been. *If you are made to appear to suffer, it can only aid your credibility.*

A sense of humor is an asset of inestimable value. Within yourself, resist any inclination to become angry, to "act smart," or to "show off." On the other hand, do not feel that you must pass up an opportunity for *effective and meaningful* repartee. Thus, respond only with statements that will enhance your credibility about the subject matter under discussion.

[33]

Resolve to be master of the situation!

If, because of an ailment, your appearance before the hearing might endanger your health or place a strain upon you, consult with your physician prior to any appearance before the hearing and discuss the matter with your lawyer.

As you testify before the committee or trial court, do not be condescending, patronizing or indulge in flattery. The government has vested these persons with a certain authority to aid in the gathering of facts; respect that authority.

Since each of you belongs to a profession that has a jargon of its own, and the triers of fact are of varying backgrounds, try to communicate in a common, more general language, the everyday language of the *intended* audience.

A doctor who testified on behalf of my client referred to "... a furuncle on the thenar surface of the right pollex." I asked him to translate this comment into ordinary English. He said, "... a boil on the fleshy part of the right thumb."

Even in some hearings that are conducted informally,

there may be discussions of certain technical rules of evidence or about the form of questions, resulting in motions to strike answers or parts of answers given by you. These technical encounters may appear incomprehensible and petty to you. You may wonder why the examiners do not want to hear your story as you want to tell it. The important thing for you to know is that these objections and motions, and any rulings upholding them, neither reflect nor imply any aspersion upon your integrity or intelligence. Do not allow them to disturb you. The lawyers and the examiners will handle these technical points of order.

It is perfectly proper for you to talk with your attorney before you act as a witness. It is proper for your attorney to confer with you, ask you questions, and suggest to you what questions you may be asked as an expert witness. *It is improper and unlawful for anyone to induce or try to induce you to testify falsely.* If one of the examiners should ask you if you talked with anyone about your testimony prior to testifying before the hearing, answer the question truthfully and without hesitation. State, if true, that no one directed or asked you to testify falsely, and that no one made any effort to influence your statements.

REMINDER No. 4. "Coaching" a witness is highly unethical and may be illegal and criminal; it may be subornation of perjury (the crime of inducing another to commit perjury). *An attorney or individual who deliberately asks you to testify about anything in which you have no knowledge is coaching.* There are zealots who believe the end justifies *any* means; this type of person has very little morality and will seek to use the expert for his own selfish or political pur-

"Coaching" a witness is highly unethical
and may be illegal and criminal.

pose. We have seen this occur in the **McCarthy** and other hearings.

Coaching is, by direct or indirect means, telling, suggesting, or indicating to a witness what testimony is desired of him, when such witness knows nothing of the substance of such testimony.

"Preparing" or rehearsing a witness, however, is an entirely different matter. Preparing is a responsibility for an attorney. One should never put a witness on the stand unless he knows exactly what will be said. The questions to be asked are practiced so that the witness will not be surprised. The *only* questions asked are to elicit truthful information. The witness should be prepared for tricky questions on cross-examination. The attorney should play the role of cross-examiner. In this exercise the witness will be relaxed. Remember, the jury listens to direct evidence, but hears the answers on cross-examination. There are some examiners, regrettably, who under the guise of "preparing" witnesses, skate the thin ice of "coaching" witnesses and rationalize doing this in the interest of their client's just cause. "Coaching," regardless of noble intentions, is never justified.

Take the material that you are now reading to the hearing with you; have it in your pocket or handbag. If the opposing counsel asks if you have been given instructions or advice on how to testify, tell him "Yes," that the instructions are in writing, that you have them with you. Produce this book and show it to the court or hearing officer.

REMINDER No. 5. Take a note pad into the hearing room with you. If testimony from another witness prompts you to communicate with your attorney, it is preferable to write him a note rather than to talk to him. You also can use your notes to remind you of matters to discuss with your attorney during a recess.

There is no way you can be tricked or embarrassed if you answer questions honestly and straightforwardly.

Take a notepad into the courtroom or hearing room.

1. Don't exaggerate or try to withhold information that you think might be unfavorable to your side.
2. Listen to the questions carefully and answer them directly; don't volunteer information.
3. If you can, answer the questions with "yes" or "no"; if you cannot, say so and give your answer.

   If you don't know the answer or don't remember, just say so; don't guess the answer.
4. Tell what you do know, but do not speculate. Don't repeat what someone else told you unless asked to do so.
5. If you don't understand the question, say so and let the examiner rephrase it. If you think you understand it, but aren't sure, you can even rephrase it yourself. For example, you might say, "If you mean such and such, then my answer is thus and so." *Don't give the impression that you are sparring with the examiner or trying to avoid answering a legitimate question.* If the question is not proper, the lawyer will object to it. **Give the lawyer time to make an objection.**

Usually, examiners will badger a witness if it appears he is not telling the truth. If an examiner does try to needle you, remain calm. That will make him look foolish. An examiner may ask you whether you have talked to anyone about your testimony. *Of course, your answer will be "yes," won't it?*

Don't drink alcohol or take tranquilizers before
you go to the court or hearing.

REMINDER No. 6. Abstain from drinking alcohol or taking tranquilizers before going to the court or hearing. These drugs won't really make you less nervous. On the contrary, they may cause you to look and sound confused.

Other Tips: Avoid distracting and annoying mannerisms such as tapping your foot or talking with your hand over your mouth. When you are off the witness stand listening to the testimony of others, refrain from any demonstration or expression of surprise, shock, disapproval, contempt, or approval.

REMINDER No. 7. As an expert witness you may be asked hypothetical questions. Hypothetical questions recite facts and other matter on which an expert witness is asked to base his opinion testimony. The witness is asked to assume, for the purposes of his or her answer, that the matter recited in the question is true, whether or not the expert

[39]

Don't daydream!

has any knowledge of that matter, and even though the expert may believe it to be false. The matter on which the expert's opinion is based is thus "made known" to you during the hearing. Hypothetical questions are discussed in detail on page 22.

Expert Witness and Trial Techniques

REMINDER No. 8. The trial plan of your lawyer should outline, in detail, the type of questions expected to be asked on cross-examination. While the entire cross-examination can rarely be planned, the general program of attack can be simulated by role playing. Often a specific line of questions can be anticipated that will bring about proper emphasis and create dramatic effect whenever possible.

At any point in the questioning (on both direct and cross-examination) where it is expected that an objection may be raised by the question or by the evidence that is offered, your lawyer should include in the trial brief a citation of law to support the propriety of the question or the admissibility of the evidence.

Some lawyers also include in their plan the substantive law applicable to the case, but that is not essential if the trial memorandum for the court has covered all the points. Trial briefs are normally required to be lodged with the trial judge. They are always required in Federal Court. All witnesses are described with a synopsis of their testimony. All

The trial plan of your lawyer should outline the
type of questions to be asked on cross-examination.

points anticipated to be raised plus legal authority to support the position are included. If it is desired to support or oppose the introduction of certain evidence on substantive grounds, a cross-reference can be made to the appropriate page in the trial memorandum.

To avoid overlooking any technical step in procedure, some counsel will take the precaution of indicating, in their notes or in the trial plan, the various motions which they anticipate making during the course of the trial. In a case tried before a jury, they will also include a tentative outline of their summation on notes to matters which they want to be sure will not be overlooked when summing up. The outline of summation will have to be changed after the evidence is in; it should be followed by a tentative draft of requests to charge (instructions to the jury) which the thorough lawyer will have prepared in advance of the trial.

Most lawyers will adjust their plans to the needs of the

particular case, to the time they can allot to planning, and to their own preferences in planning.

The best of plans can often be destroyed. I had a criminal case to defend and my plan included an iron-clad alibi. The last witness I put on the stand answered as follows:

Q. When did you last talk to my client?
A. *This morning when he asked me to lie about where he was on the night of the crime.*

Although your lawyers try the case from a "trial brief for counsel," from notes in a loose leaf notebook, or from a memorandum pad, every lawyer who undertakes to try a case should have a trial plan that has prepared the lawyer to the fullest extent possible under the circumstances. What has been said about counsel's trial plan may serve as a guide to those matters that should be considered in advance, regardless of the form of planning adopted by counsel.

Final Preparation for Trial or Public Hearing

REMINDER No. 9. Final preparation with each witness should include a preview of the facts to which the witness will testify on examination.

If there are any discrepancies, or apparent discrepancies, they should be brought out into the open, discussed, and, if possible, reconciled or, if not, explained.

Preparing a Witness for Direct Examination. You, as a

Final preparation with each witness should include a
preview of the relevant facts.

witness, should be familiar with any exhibits which you
will have to identify, interpret, or testify about during the
course of the examination. A witness should understand the
importance of each link of the chain. Your lawyer should
notify you that certain exhibits will be introduced at a certain point and the notification should be accompanied by
an explanation as to the reason why the exhibit will be offered.

The witness should understand the aim of the examiner,
the implication of the questions and the nature of the answer which each of the questions seeks to elicit. You will be
an effective and cooperative witness if you use your own
language and *know what you are talking about.*

The rule with regard to preparing an expert witness who
will give an opinion is quite different from that relating to
witnesses who will testify only as to facts. Your lawyer must
determine the exact language of any technical or hypothetical questions and the proper language with which to
respond to those questions. The proper *word* may be extremely important.

When questioning experts, the omission of a necessary word, the insertion of a superfluous word, or a slight variation in expression may make so much of a difference in the mind of an expert who wishes to be exact, that the expert cannot give the answer which the expert anticipated. There are few witnesses who are sufficiently skillful to be able to suggest the necessary correction in the question, and even a witness who is capable of doing so may not find the opportunity.

If there are any discrepancies or apparent discrepancies between the testimony of the witness and documentary evidence, or between your testimony and a statement which you had made in a document, you will need to reconcile the differences or explain your error.

Do not volunteer an answer, or be talkative with opposing counsel. You must answer truthfully and without hesitation any question about your past history, admit readily your signature or handwriting, or the identity of a document. Unless there is a real doubt in your mind, admit readily errors or inaccuracies in your testimony and correct them at the first opportunity. It is important to answer promptly and truthfully.

REMINDER NO. 10. It is dangerous to have an impertinent, belligerent or rebellious attitude, which may be used to advantage by a skillful opponent.

Your lawyer must be careful to observe your habits of speech. Many an honest witness makes a poor impression because the witness is not definite in his language, although his knowledge warrants certainty. Some witnesses, in an ef-

Don't be impertinent, belligerent, or unresponsive.

fort to be fair, go to the other extreme and assume facts about which they have no personal knowledge or recollection; **either extreme is dangerous.**

Do not guess, nor answer "I assume so" or "I believe so" or "That is probably the fact," but do say "I do not know" when you do not in fact know the answer, and do say "I do not remember" when you do not in fact remember. Say "Yes" when you mean "Yes" and not "I think so" nor "I believe so," and "No" when you mean "No" and not "I don't think so" or "I don't believe so."

REMINDER No. 11. Any witness who is hard of hearing or whose understanding of the English language is inadequate should be warned to be certain that he has heard and understood every word in the question before answering, and to ask that the question be repeated or explained if necessary.

REMINDER No. 12. Be advised that there are certain types of "catch" questions.

Most famous is the question: *"Did you discuss the case with anyone?*" It is amazing how many witnesses will answer that they did not, although they spent hours in conference with a lawyer. Sometimes the answer is due to an incorrect assumption that discussions with the lawyer are not included in the question. Frequently the witness labors under the false belief that the question implies some moral rebuke concerning any discussion of the case.

The witness must be warned against a really tricky question such as: "Are you being paid for your testimony?" The catchword is "testimony." The unwary witness may answer "Yes," whereas the proper answer to that question would be "No," because "payment for testimony" imports much more than payment for the time spent in court or reimbursement

If you don't hear or understand the question,
ask for a repeat.

The opposing attorney may ask a catchy or tricky question.

for loss or expenses incurred as a result of attendance at the trial. **The truthfully prepared answer is: "No, I am not paid for my testimony; I am paid for my time."**

Presenting the Evidence

Qualifying an Expert

REMINDER No. 13. It is essential to qualify an expert witness. Whether the witness be an anthropologist, a lawyer, an accountant, an economist, a cartographer, a biologist, an engineer, an archaeologist, a physicist, or any other type of witness called to offer expert testimony, the expert's qualifications should be fully recorded. Your attorney will ask questions to demonstrate to the jury that you

It is essential to qualify an expert witness, whether that
witness is a chemist, surgeon, teacher, engineer . . .

are a highly trained individual. The questions will include references to your formal training in college, specialized schools, degrees, publications, honors, amount of time spent in a particular job, and the like. *Remember, anyone can be an expert witness.*

Purposes of Examination. Generally speaking, the purposes of examination are described as follows:

1. To obtain helpful testimony from the witness that will directly support the contention of the examiner's position, or support the contention indirectly by invalidating the effect of the witness' testimony or of other evidence presented.

2. To discredit testimony of the witness by eliciting contradictions, modifications or retractions of material testimony previously given, or explanations of such testimony which by its nature is so incredible as to cast doubt upon its validity.

Even if the witness does not modify his testimony, this type of examination may be used to point out selected facts in such sequence and with such emphasis as to discredit the testimony by logical inferences.

The scientific testimony of a witness may also be discredited or weakened by eliciting, on examination, answers which create doubt about the physical circumstances which enabled him to observe the facts, his powers of observation, and his ability to recollect facts accurately.

3. To discredit the witness by eliciting contradictions, modifications, retractions, or incredible explanations as to collateral matters, or to elicit admissions as to a discreditable history, such as a criminal conviction, or disbarment, thus impairing his or her credibility.

The first attack to weaken an opponent's expert is always to ask questions which show his direct or indirect pecuniary interest in the subject, his relationship to the party on whose behalf he testifies, his friendship for that party, his hostility to the opposing party, or other prejudices. In some cases it is possible to discredit the witness by questioning his motives in connection with the subject matter of the case.

4. To discredit a witness one often uses the technique of **impeachment.** Impeachment of a witness occurs by testimony of another person concerning contradictory statements made orally by the witness to that person, or by the introduction in evidence of prior writings or recorded sworn testimony of the witness inconsistent with his testimony.

5. To lay the foundation for an objection to incompetent testimony when the incompetency does not appear from the preliminary questions asked on direct examination, from the answers of the witness, or from any other part of the record as it then stands. This is often accomplished by use of an expert with superior credentials, education, or experience compared to the expert for the other side. It allows a comparison of opinion based on unequal qualifications.

Discrediting the Testimony

REMINDER No. 14. **A method of discrediting testimony is cross-examination, forcing the witness to contradict himself, to modify or retract former statements, or to offer inadequate explanations.** An example of the above is the following story.

The witness was convincing. No one on the jury doubted that her statements were true. She had testified that fault was entirely the defendant's.

I asked:

Q. What relationship exists between you and the plaintiff?

A. *I'm her mother.*

Contradiction by Prior Testimony. If the examiner has prior testimony of the witness recorded in the minutes of a hearing, or of an examination of a prior hearing, which contradicts in any material respect testimony given by that witness during the pending hearing, the examiner has the right to read to the witness any part of that prior testimony which varies from the current testimony.

Don't get upset when the opposing attorney may try to discredit your testimony. Keep calm and stick to the truth.

The examiner may merely ask the witness if he gave such prior testimony, and rely on the obvious prior inconsistent testimony to contradict the current testimony. Or, having called the witness' attention to the variation, the examiner may ask the witness whether, in view of the prior testimony, the answer which the witness currently gave should be changed. The witness may then correct his present testimony on the theory that he erred in his current recollection. In that way, a complete retraction or modification may be obtained.

The witness, on the other hand, may seek to explain the variation. The examiner may also invite such explanation if the examiner feels certain the explanation will be *incredible* (unbelievable). In either event, if the explanation is inadequate, the effect desired by the examiner will have been obtained.

Discrediting the Witness

REMINDER No. 15. If the attack on the credibility of a witness is based upon the witness' former criminal conduct, the witness may be properly asked whether the witness was ever convicted of a crime, but not whether the witness was ever arrested or indicted, for the latter do not carry any presumption of wrongdoing.

A witness may be asked point-blank whether the witness committed a particular crime, or was guilty of any other conduct which may affect character and credibility, but if the witness denies it, the cross-examiner is bound by the answer and may not offer evidence to contradict the witness.

The reason for the distinction between the conviction which has not been reversed on appeal is *res judicata* (a matter already decided by judicial authority). The commission of a crime that is denied would require a trial within a trial. The court will not permit offering any evidence in support of such a collateral attack.

It is improper in some jurisdictions to attack credibility by proof of prior criminal conduct, unless the crime is one related to truthfulness, such as theft, embezzlement, perjury, or acts of moral turpitude.

Personal Interest or Bias. A less severe but more frequent type of examination is addressed to weakening of credibility of the witness by showing his pecuniary interest in the outcome of the suit, his relationship to the parties, his friendship for one party or hostility toward the other, or bias caused by any other circumstance.

Examinations as to Relationship or Friendship. Generally, examination as to the relationship of a witness to a party will be brief. It is not uniformly effective in impairing the credibility of a witness but should be brought out on an examination for its worth in helping to evaluate the testimony of the witness.

Examination as to Hostility, Bias or Prejudice. A party may show that a witness is hostile by proving acts or declarations of the witness, either out of the witness' own mouth or from others. The witness may, therefore, be asked on ex-

The witness may be properly asked whether the witness was ever convicted of a crime, but not whether the witness was ever arrested or indicted.

amination about any hostile acts or declarations on the witness' part which would show hostility to the party against whom the witness is testifying. If he denies such acts or declarations, he may be contradicted by the testimony of other witnesses.

Questionable Conduct of Witness. Occasionally a witness is vulnerable because of his own conduct in connection with the subject matter. The witness can, on such occasions, be attacked by examination which seeks to focus attention upon reprehensible conduct on his part.

Sometimes the conduct may cast doubt upon his story. In such case, if the examiner can succeed in obtaining admissions from the witness as to his conduct, his credibility as a witness will be impaired. This is always the case when an informer is used in a criminal action.

There are also occasions when the conduct of the witness may not have a direct bearing upon the truthfulness of his story or upon the issues in the case, but his actions may be such as to render him suspect and therefore unworthy of credibility.

Examining Expert Witnesses

REMINDER No. 16. Expert witnesses are not only experts in their own particular fields, but with frequent appearances in court they also become "expert" at being witnesses. They develop, in some cases, a remarkable ability to speak around a question without directly answering it. They may start the answer directly enough, but soon switch off to some dissertation which has no direct applicability.

Generally speaking, **the handling of an expert witness upon examination presents no particular problem in the method of preparation by the lawyer.** Here, the rule of thorough preparation applies to the fullest degree. The examiner is going outside of his own particular field. **The examiner will be called upon to match wits with you in your chosen field.** This would seem a hopeless task, but while the inquiry in your field proceeds, it will usually be confined to a narrow corner of that field, and adequate preparation by the lawyer is feasible.

In one case a doctor testified about injuries to the plaintiff. All symptoms had subsided except a persistent stiffness in the left big toe. The preparation focused on one joint and expertise was obtained in a short time. All other injuries did not require preparation.

Any person of average intelligence and education could select a chapter from any law book and, in a comparatively short time, master that chapter. One would likely know more about that narrow subject than would the ordinary lawyer. So it is with any other subject. Without very much effort a lawyer can read all that has been published in medical books about a certain disease, its cause and its treatment. In like manner, he may master narrow fields of engineering, chemistry, or other sciences. The lawyer is usually aided in doing so by the experts he has chosen.

With "expert" witnesses, the examiner will attempt to dominate the examination, to keep control of the course of the examination, and to insist that the answers be directed to the questions as presented.

In conclusion, it is well to remember that the writings of recognized authorities upon any given subject, in any branch of the sciences, are ordinarily admissible as evidence.

Points to Remember

1. Dress conservatively for your hearing or court appearance.
2. Be honest with your answers.
3. Be master of the situation. Let nothing deter you.
4. Coaching the witness can be illegal. Discussion of the facts is permissible.
5. Be studious, take notes.
6. Don't cloud your mind with alcohol or drugs.
7. Listen to the question. Don't daydream.
8. Your attorney will prepare a master strategy.
9. Preparation of the expert witness is permissible.
10. Being rowdy or obnoxious doesn't help the expert witness.
11. If you don't hear the question, ask for a repeat.
12. Be careful! The sly examiner will try to trap you.
13. The professionals have to be qualified as expert witnesses.
14. The opposing examiner will try to discredit your testimony.

15. It may be legal to ask whether you have been convicted of a felony, but not whether you were ever arrested or indicted, since the latter do not carry any presumption of wrongdoing.
16. The know-it-all witness usually gets stumped by a sharp examiner.

NOTES

NOTES

NOTES